How to add the "WOW" Experience To your Customer Service In 3 easy steps

Dr. James Ortman

ISBN:1482584972
ISBN-13:9781482584974

To all my Maize and Blue Event Staff Team Members Who in
Relentlessly Striving to make Michigan Athletics the Leaders and
Best in every way provide Exceptional Experiences for Every Guest!
This is what makes us proud to be Wolverines!
GO BLUE!

CONTENTS

PREFACE

Please use this book as a workbook. I hope you will have it with you every day, like a diary. I have designed the book to leave room on every page for you to take "Aha" notes as you read and think about all the possibilities. I have also left blank pages for you to begin your process of writing a customer service book that will help you develop "WOW EXPERIENCES" that will meet your needs. All the new technics and ideas you will learn can be used not only while you work but every moment of every day. Throughout the book, I will be asking key questions about how you or your organization is handling certain customer service situations.

Have you ever told anyone to treat others the way they would want to be treated? This used to be the standard customer service approach, but as our culture changes and we become more diverse, our approach must change in order to not offend anyone.

WHAT ARE "WOW" EXPERIENCES?

Just what are "WOW" experiences and why do we need them anyway? If we take the time to think about it there are two types of "WOW" experiences, the amazing "WOW" I can't believe that just happened or the negative "WOW" I can't believe that just happened. I'm going to share with you a negative "WOW," I can't believe that just happened experience that is the basis for this book. This is a short story of what happened.

We have lived in the same small town for over 30 years, and like every small town, everyone in the community knows each other by their first names. There is a general store where many of us greet each other and of course, share the latest news. My wife called out to me while I was in the yard working and asked me to walk up town to purchase a can of soup at the general store. So I grabbed the dogs and their leashes, and we headed up to the general store. When I entered the store, I saw the owner's wife standing at the cash register talking with someone. She did not make eye contact with me or even say hello. I didn't think much of it as I proceeded to the soup isle. I grabbed the can of soup and went directly to the checkout. The owner's wife was still talking with the lady, so I just sat the can of soup down on the counter to wait until she was done talking. The owner's wife snatched the can of soup off the counter and proceeded to ring up the sale while still having a conversation with the lady. At this point, I could tell the lady was not a customer and was looking for a donation for a fundraising event. I handed the owner's wife a five dollar bill for a dollar and a half purchase. She handed me the change and set the can of soup in front of me and never said one word to me and never skipped a beat with the lady. I picked up the can of soup and walked out the door, and the first thing I said was, "WOW" I can't believe that. As I was walking home, I was talking to my dogs about everything that was wrong with that situation, and they listened well. When I got home I started to tell my wife about what had happened, and she said well you couldn't do anything about it, that's just the way some people are. So I began thinking about how a can of soup could cost that business owner a lot of lost sales because of poor customer service. I won't point out all the things that went wrong, but you can use this as a case study if you want. So the question is what type of "WOW" experiences are you providing for your customers?

This book is going to concentrate on the positive "WOW" experiences.

"WOW" experiences are when we provide above what is expected customer service, and the customer literally says "WOW, I didn't expect that" or something similar. At some point, we have all had "WOW" experiences. But how do they happened and why do they happen is what we need to understand.

We can no longer just satisfy our customers with

providing good customer service. We need to "WOW" them every single day. It is a simple truth: customers continue to do business with organizations that deliver on what they promise and who have treated them fairly while continuing to do the little things that the competition does not do.

You have far more potential to develop long lasting relationships and future business success by managing customer expectations in a consistent way. This sounds simple, in fact, you might be saying to yourself, we already do this, but do you?

Here are a few questions to think about.

Does your entire organization understand your position when it comes to customer satisfaction?

Do you have a company manual that has specific and measurable goals for your customer service?

Do you reward your staff for providing great customer service?

How much training do you provide for the people directly responsible for your customer service?

How often are your customer services policies reviewed and updated to meet current market conditions?

How many letters have you received from your customers that say "WOW" thanks for....?

By now you probably have some "Aha" notes; great you are on your way to creating "WOW" experiences. You are consciously beginning to assess where you are as an organization, a manager, and an individual.

Here is a simple but important "WOW" experience a friend shared with me.

While out of town in early December, my wife and I had the dreadful experience of a dead battery. What made it worse was that this happened on a Sunday morning. We were suddenly faced with spending all day trying to get ourselves back on the road. But surprisingly, one call to our roadside assistance provider did the trick. Within forty minutes, the driver met us, jumped the battery, diagnosed the problem, replaced the battery, and we were on our way.

This is service beyond expectation, the "WOW Experience." This is what we constantly need to train our staff we want and need to provide. In this day of strong competition and high expectations, service is everything, and the 'WOW Experience can separate you from your competition.

STEP 1: HAVING THE RIGHT MINDSET

Providing "WOW" experiences takes a particular mindset and a conscious effort by the customer service person. This is easy, but hard. It is hard because it calls for change in your current habits, but it is easy because when you learn the new skills, you will perform them without even thinking about it. We have to understand how we can create the "WOW" experience with every customer. When we find that we don't know something, we're often motivated to learn more. We make a conscience effort to learn. However if we are unaware of our not knowing, there is little we can do about it. We just can't give our customer service people a couple of "WOW" experience examples and expect them to understand how to create the "WOW" experience or even to be consciously aware without the proper training.

One of the first steps on the journey to providing "WOW" experiences is acquiring new skills and to be consciously aware of what we don't know. That's right what we don't know is what we need to know. This discovery can be uncomfortable, as can be the experience of not being very good at what you're trying to do. When people first start to learn they will want to fall back to old habits. We basically don't like to change what we are comfortable with. In fact, some of your customer service people will say there is nothing wrong with what they currently are doing. They will say the system they are using is just fine. This is a critical stage when it's much easier to give up and go back to old habits then to form new ones. If we are not willing to understand why we must change then the competition wins.

The Organization's Culture

Focusing on building and sustaining an organizational culture is a way of showing that people are the organization's most valuable asset. But sometimes a change is required for better efficiency and productivity. Companies, which have embraced organizational culture change, see a definite increase in their employee engagement, the attraction of new customers and boosting their revenues. A good organizational culture should be nurtured and should be kept intact towards company's goals, mission, and vision. The organization culture is like an outer shell of the egg, which acts as a protective shield that helps to keep intact the integrity of the company. I personally feel that an employee who believes in values and culture of an organization is much more valuable than the bottom line; as the bottom line can be generated once again but to lose an efficient team member and win them back is much more difficult in the current business world.

A former employee once worked for a medium-sized call center with 200 or so employees. The culture involved employees that distrusted upper management and as a result had low morale and constant issues (in some form). When a new manager came in the culture slowly changed (over a period of 2 years). Her demeanor, fairness, and transparent nature were the reason for the change. She was very up front with changes that could be made and provide "WOW" experiences. She had the ability to share and teach how she believed her management team should act. She was very consistent and never expected more out of her team than she was willing to do. She often worked out on the floor and asked for input directly from "her team." She had a way of making everyone feel included and was first to celebrate the changes that helped the employee to provide the "WOW" experiences and over time she was able to win their trust. As a result, the morale issues faded and the team became more efficient. It was like watching an old beat up pickup truck restored to all its former glory.

There is a need to create clarity for all employees regarding customer service quality policies and customer satisfaction targets when implementing the "WOW" experience. It is not enough to pay lip-service to these ideals and to expect success in attaining them. The starting point must be established to identify what has to be achieved in customer satisfaction to implement specific market strategies, and to position the company against the competition in a particular market. It is unlikely that performing what is needed will be free from cost. We need to take a realistic view of the time required and the actual cost of implementation in aligning the internal market with the external market.

Internal processes and barriers suggest the need to consider both the inner and external markets faced in implementing customer satisfaction measurement and management systems. To ignore the internal market is to risk actually damaging the company's capacity to achieve and improve customer satisfaction in the external market. If for example, management uses customer feedback in a negative and coercive way, then it may reduce employee enthusiasm for customer service, or create 'game-playing' behavior where people compete for 'Brownie points' in the system at the expense of both the company and the customer. This said, we have also to recognize not just the complementarity between internal and external markets, but the potential for conflict of interest. Achieving target levels of customer service and satisfaction may require managers and employees to change the way they do things and to make sacrifices they do not want to make. This may take more than mere advocacy or management threat.

Related to the above argument, recognizing the internal market suggests that there may be a need for a structured and planned internal customer service program to achieve the effective implementation of customer satisfaction measurement and management. This has been described as 'marketing our customers to our employees' and can be built into the implementation process to address the needs of the internal customer and to confront the types of internal procession barrier we have encountered. Other departments might not support your "WOW" experiences approach to customer service. They may not recognize the need or benefits.

Also related to the recognition of the internal market is the need to question the relationship between internal and external customer satisfaction. This can be discussed with executives using the structure. This suggests four possible scenarios that result when internal and external customer satisfaction are compared:

(a) Synergy, which is what we hope for, when internal and external customer satisfaction are high, and we see them as sustainable and self-regenerating. As one manager explained it: 'I know that we are winning on customer service when my operational staff come to me and complain about how I am getting in their way in providing "WOW" experiences, and tell me to get my act together!' This is the 'happy customers and happy employees' situation, assumed by many to be obvious and easily achieved.

(b) Coercion is where we achieve high levels of external customer satisfaction by changing the behavior of employees through management direction and control systems. In the short term, this may be the only option, but it may be very difficult and expensive to sustain this position in the longer term, and we give up flexibility for control. This style can challenge providing "WOW" experiences.

(c) Alienation is where we have low levels of satisfaction internally and externally, and we are likely to be highly vulnerable to competitive attack on service quality, and to the instability in our competitive capabilities produced by low staff morale and high staff turnover. "WOW" experiences are not present.

(d) Internal euphoria is where we have high levels of satisfaction in the internal market, but this does not translate into external customer satisfaction – for example, if internal socialization and group cohesiveness actually shut out the paying customer in the external market. These scenarios are exaggerated but have provided a useful way of confronting these issues with executives.

A critical mistake is to ignore the real costs and challenges in sustaining "WOW" experiences and high service quality levels and the limitation which may exist in a company's capabilities for improving customer satisfaction levels. While advocacy is widespread and the appeal is obvious, achieving the potential benefits requires more planning and attention to implementation realities than is suggested by the existing conventional process.

WE DO NOT KNOW WHAT WE DO NOT KNOW

BECOMING CONSCIOUSLY AWARE

Creating and providing "WOW" experiences means we need to begin thinking in a different way. We need to change our thought process. Put yourself in the shoes of your customer. What could the customer service person do extra that would cause you to say "WOW"?

Ok, you had to consciously think about it. It just didn't pop into your head. You just didn't do it automatically did you? Don't worry, once you understand the process you will unconsciously become aware of ways before they happen. You will be able to anticipate and react before you even consciously think about it. But a word of caution, things will come to mind so easily for you, the common reaction is, gee, why didn't they think of that? Remember you were an unconscious incompetent at one point.

The Conscious Competence Ladder is a popular and intuitive approach which can be attributed to many different possible originators, that helps us to manage our own emotions during a sometimes dispiriting learning process. More than this, it helps us to be more in touch with the emotions of the people we are teaching, so we can better coach them through the learning process. We also become more aware of the customer's emotions. The reason I am suggesting this approach over other approaches is you will find yourself using this approach in all areas of your life once you consciously understand why we do what we do.

With this approach, consciousness is the first step towards gaining knowledge and understanding how to create the "WOW" experiences. We must have a consciousness toward our customer's needs and expectations. To learn new skills and to gain knowledge we need to be conscious of what we do and don't know. We also need to be conscious of what is happening around us. For example, there are many things that happen around us every day that we take for granted and accept them because we are not consciously thinking about them. Learning to drive your car was a conscious effort right? Now you jump in and before you know it you are at your destination without much thought consciously, but in your unconscious part of your mind, you were going through several steps to arrive at your destination. This type of thinking allows you to create the "WOW" experience with very little effort.

Competence is your ability to do things. You may be highly competent in one area, but have no skill in another. Your competence level will depend on the task or job at hand. Good customer service models are positive attitudes, good communication skills and customer focused. We have all heard and understand customer service representatives should be friendly and courteous while smiling and being helpful. This is all good if we are consciously aware but what if they aren't? What if your customer service representative is going through all the steps that they have been trained to do and they provided good customer service, but you are not getting a "WOW" response from customers? This is where you need to evaluate your customer service goals and expectations. In the last six months how many letters, phone calls or emails have you received from customers praising your customer service?

Letters-

Phone Calls-

Emails-

Now compare this number to the number of total customers you provide a service to. Well, what did you find out? Very seldom will a customer make an effort to contact an organization to praise them unless there has been a "WOW" experience. The idea is that as you build expertise in new areas of customer service creating the "WOW" experience, you move from "unconscious incompetence" to "conscious incompetence" and then to "conscious competence," finally reaching "unconscious competence. These are explained in the following steps.

Notes

Conscious Competence Ladder of Learning

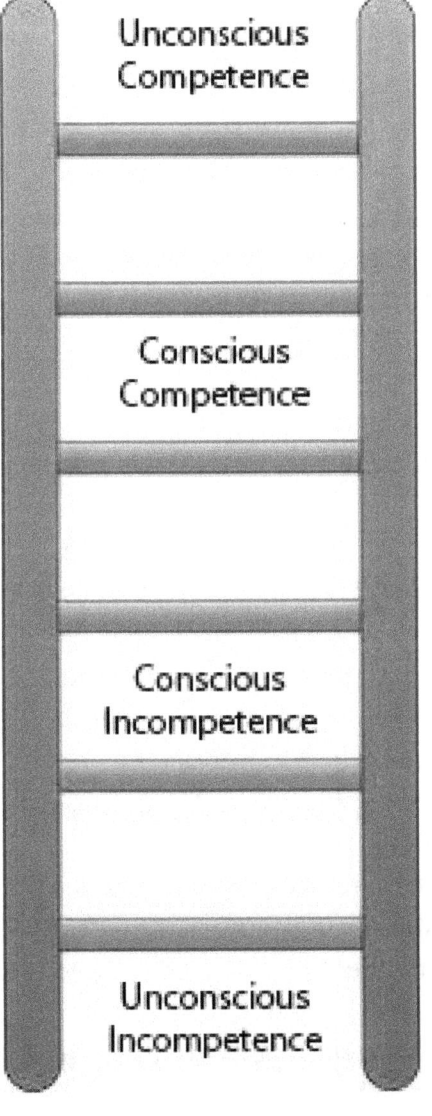

•Unconscious Competence: Although this is the ideal state, you'll need to make sure that people avoid complacency, and stay abreast of their fields. You may also need to remind people how difficult it was to reach this state so that they are tolerant of people at the Conscious Incompetence stage!

•Conscious Competence: At this stage, you need to keep people focused on the effective performance of the task, and give plenty of opportunities for them to get practice. Challenge them to create new "WOW" experiences.

•Conscious Incompetence: During this stage, you'll need to provide plenty of encouragement, tolerate mistakes appropriately, and do what you can to help people improve.

• Unconscious Incompetence: At the beginning of the process, they may be unaware of their own lack of competence, and may need to be made gently aware of how much they need to learn.

Step 1 - Unconscious Incompetence State of Thinking

We need, to begin with the understanding of how we think and why we make the decisions we do.

• We must understand the customer service person is not aware of the existence or relevance of the skill area to get the "WOW" response. This is why many organizations use some type of script. It might be faster to train a person to use a script then teach them to use this approach but the results can and will be well worth the time and effort.

• Next, the customer service person is not aware that they have a particular deficiency in the area concerned. This is when we need to give examples why this is so important for the "WOW" experience.

• The customer service person might deny the relevance or usefulness of the new skill. "Everything is fine so why change anything"?

• The customer service person must become conscious of their incompetence before the development of the new skills and learning can begin.

• The aim of the customer service person and the trainer or teacher is to move the person into the conscious competence stage, by demonstrating the skill or ability and the benefit that it will bring to the person's effectiveness while providing the "WOW" experience.

An example would be the customer service person states "I said everything on the script sheet" so I am giving good service, right? Well, the script sheet is a guide, and sometimes it does not fit the situation leaving an awkward situation between the customer service person and the customer.

Here is an example of creating a "WOW" experience that might help the current state of thinking.

I was working with a guest services team member when a request was made for a wheelchair assist. Normally the guest services team member will greet the guests at the front door of the arena. This time I suggested the guest services team member greet the guest outside the arena at the guest's car in the parking lot. This could be a "WOW" experience all by itself, but let's continue. As they were making their way around the arena, the guest asked if they could stop at a nearby water fountain for a sip of water. The guest commented they were very parched. (This is a key word to remember). Upon arrival at their seat, the guest thanked the guest services team member for such good service. The guest services team member said you're welcome with a smile. As we left, I asked the guest services team member how we could create a "WOW" experience. They thought we already had by going to the parking lot and assisting the guest (the guest services person is in the Unconscious Incompetence State of Thinking). I stated you gave good service, and it could be a small "WOW" because we went to the parking lot but now let's consciously think how we can give a better "WOW" experience. Recall the guest making a comment "They were very parched?" Usually, a sip of water is not sufficient to quench the thirst from being parched, right? Now consciously put yourself in the guest situation, in about 20 minutes you would possibly want some more water. Let's get a glass of ice water and take it to the guest. At the same time, we can check to see how they're doing. The guest services team member never considered this; however, it made perfect sense after we discussed why we were doing this. As we approached the seating area, the guest saw us and was very surprised and full of praise for thinking about them, and yes they really wanted a drink of water. I asked the guest services team member if there's anything else we should consider doing for the guest? They suggested checking back with the guest during intermission in case they needed assistance to the restroom. Why would we consider this? That's right because of the amount of water that the guest has consumed. Once again, the guest was surprised and thankful. Two very simple things that the guest services team member provided for the guest created the "WOW" experience. The guest services team member has gone from the Unconscious Incompetence State of Thinking (step 1) to Conscious Incompetence State of Thinking (step 2). This was all possible because the guest services team member listened to what the guest was saying and consciously anticipated what the guests' future needs might be.

Take a moment and consciously think about a recent situation that you were in either as a customer or providing some type of service.

What could have been done to create a "WOW" experience?

Step 2 - Conscious Incompetence State of Thinking

•At this stage, the customer service person becomes aware of the existence and relevance of the skill to create the "WOW" experience. Things begin to click, and there will be many "AHA" moments.

• The customer service person is therefore also aware of their deficiency in this area, ideally by attempting or trying to use the skill. This is where we need to provide encouragement and reinforce that it is ok to make mistakes while we learn these new skills.

• The customer service person realizes that by improving their skill or ability in this area, their effectiveness will improve. We need to be ready to catch them applying the new skills and offer words of encouragement. This is a time to help celebrate and offer a reward. The reward can be a simple comment like "Great Job" or "Way to go." As we know each person will react differently to the words of encouragement so make sure you are using what best fits your situation.

• Ideally, the customer service person has a measure of the extent of their deficiency in the relevant skill, and a measure of what level of skill is required for their own competence. As the successes begin to emerge and the "WOW" experience happens, keep a log of what actually made the difference. This will prove to be very valuable as we make progress toward the Unconscious Competence State of Thinking.

• The customer service person ideally makes a commitment to learning and practice the new skill and to move to the 'conscious competence' stage. Now that we have had some success we need to maintain a balance between providing "WOW" experiences from the beginning or first contact to the end or conclusion.

Here is an example of how a person wanted to provide the "WOW" experience but because they were not at the Conscious Competence State of Thinking yet did not think the situation completely through.

A couple approached the ticket window to purchase tickets for the evening's event. The gentleman had a mobility challenge, his foot was wrapped, and he was walking with crutches. The event was sold out, so the concourse area was very crowded. The supervisor of ticket scanners located at the main entrance noticed the couple and asked if they would like a wheelchair. The couple responded to the ticket scanner supervisor with a very excited and relieved yes they would like assistance. Normally the supervisor would use his radio and call Guest Services who have wheelchairs available and provide assistance for the customers. Although the ticket scanner supervisor had a radio and could have contacted Guest services for assistance, he took it upon himself to walk to the Guest services counter and obtain the wheelchair to help the couple. Although this demonstrates the extra effort to help the customer, it did take extra time to the ticket scanning supervisor to obtain the wheelchair, and he also left his area unsupervised for that period of time not to mention the guest were alone waiting. Once he obtained the wheelchair, he assisted the guest to their seats, which was located halfway around the arena concourse. Once again, this was extending extra customer service. It also took the ticket scanning supervisor away from his responsible duties. The supervisor is in the Conscious Incompetence State of Thinking. He is aware of the existence and relevance of the skill to create the "WOW" experience. One of the Guest services team members noticed the ticket scanning supervisor taking the wheelchair. The Guest Services team member wondered if arrangements had been made for assistance for the couple after the event was concluded. The Guest services team member proceeded to the ticket scanning supervisor's area of responsibility and asks him if any arrangements were made with the couple for assistance after the event. His response was no; he figured they would just leave the wheelchair at one of the exits. This is a very common mistake that is made by someone that is in the Conscious Incompetence State of Thinking. They use the new skills they have to create a "WOW" experience but because they are still developing new skills they are not aware of the bigger picture. In this case the follow-up with the guest during the event and after the event. The Guest services team member obtained the seating information from the ticket scanning supervisor and went to see the couple. The Guest services team member asked if they needed anything and assured the couple that a team member would be available at the end of the event to assist them. This is Conscious Competence State of Thinking. We are able to consciously see the complete "WOW" experience before it happens. We are anticipating what could happen next and can react to the situation.

It is important to reward the ticket scanner supervisor with words of encouragement and use the opportunity to make suggestions how they could expand on the "WOW" experience. Avoid any negative criticism how they left their area unsupervised. Use questions or statements to help get them to see how they could have been more efficient. An example could be, I'm sorry for missing your radio call. Pause, and see how they answer you. The response could be, I didn't call, I know you are busy or It was no problem I thought I could take care of it. With either response, you will know how to proceed.

Think of a recent situation that you experienced where the customer service was great to a certain point, and then you were in limbo, it felt incomplete. What do you think could have been done differently to make you feel satisfied?

What could have been done to create the "WOW" experience?

Notes

Dr. James Ortman

Notes

Step 3 - Conscious Competence State of Thinking

• This is when the customer service person achieves conscious competence in a skill when they can perform it reliably at will. At this stage new ideas and the recognition of possibilities are abundant. This is also a time when we can become frustrated with those who do not have the same newly formed skills as we do. You might even say to yourself "gee why don't they ….." This is common because you are developing the new skills and they don't understand what you now know.

• The customer service person will need to concentrate and think in order to perform this skill. At this point practicing simple acts of kindness can help. We are becoming consciously aware of many different possibilities. The blinders are off, and as we begin to analyze our surroundings we will begin to notice the little things like lending a hand to someone who is trying to carry too much, and they are showing signs of a struggle or at the store checkout when the person behind you only has one item, and you have several. You say to them "why don't you go ahead of me" their first reaction will be a shocked expression on their face. When they say thank you be sure to say "it's my pleasure" not sure not a problem. We will discuss this later in using the right words. At the same time, you have left an impression on the check-out operator who

I am sure if you ask them they do not see this type of behavior very often.

• The customer service person can perform this new skill without assistance. We are consciously looking for ways big or small to make a "WOW" experience.

• The customer service person will not reliably perform the skill unless consciously thinking about it - the skill is not yet 'second nature' or 'automatic.' But this is ok because every "WOW" experience helps support the new skill. The customer service person is experiencing positive feedback and is building confidence.

• The customer service person should be able to demonstrate the skill to another person but is unlikely to be able to teach it well to another person. If possible create teams of support, and they can share experiences.

• The customer service person should ideally continue to practice the new skill, and if appropriate commit to becoming 'unconsciously competent' at the new skill.

• Practice is the single most effective way to move from step 3 to 4. By now you have experienced this new found skill positively affecting both your personal and professional life experiences.

Take a couple of minutes and write down a recent "WOW" experience from your personal life and professional life. Use these experience to share with others.

Personal "WOW" experience:

Professional "WOW" experience:

Notes

Notes

Step 4 - Unconscious Competence State of Thinking

Sometimes you will hear on the news about people performing random acts of kindness. People take the time to think what they can do to help someone. The Unconscious Competence State of Thinking is where things come to mind spontaneously just by observing a situation.

• The skill becomes so practiced that it enters the unconscious parts of the brain - it becomes 'second nature' to you. Your customer service representative will continuously be looking for ways to provide every customer with the "WOW" experience

• Common examples are driving your car, playing sports activities, listening and communicating. We do all these things without consciously thinking about them.

• It becomes possible for certain skills to be performed while doing something else, for example, knitting while watching TV or driving your car.

• The customer service person might now be able to teach others in the skill concerned, although after some time of being unconsciously competent the person might actually have difficulty in explaining exactly how they do it -

the skill has become largely instinctual.

• This is why there is a need for long-standing unconscious competence to be checked periodically against new standards.

The Conscious Competence Ladder helps us in two ways: It gives us reassurance when we need it, and it helps us coach others through a sometimes difficult learning process.

During the Conscious Incompetence phase, we have the reassurance that while things are difficult and frustrating right now, things will get much better in the future. And when we're at the stage of Unconscious Competence, the model reminds us to value the skills we have so painstakingly acquired.

As an approach to coaching others, it reminds us that people may be moving through these steps as they learn the new skills we're trying to teach them:

An exercise I find helpful when I coach with different organizations is to do a walk around the organization with a fresh set of eyes to see things that we become blind to because we observe them every day. As we walk, I will ask questions about things I observed such as hand written notes that have been re-taped on the wall a number of times, do people still read and need them? You can and should do this on a scheduled basis. This can be a fun exercise to get the staff involved and get them consciously thinking and of course have a reward for the person who wins.

A word of caution, when you reach the Unconscious Competence State of Thinking, it can become frustrating when working with someone who has not achieved this level of thinking. Things seem to come to mind with ease, and you find yourself thinking gee isn't it obvious? When in all reality it isn't because they have not achieved the same level of thinking or have had the same training. A pro-active customer service representative anticipates the needs of the customer and follows through. This is also true with team members, family, and friends.

Notes

DO YOU HAVE THE RIGHT PEOPLE?

It's not surprising that people who are great at customer service love to be around people. One of the first things you must look for in people is whether or not they are passionate about helping others. Next are they coachable and trainable? Are they willing to accept changes, make changes and be happy? Creating "WOW" experiences are not easy at first but once we develop a Conscious Competence State of Thinking it is fun and rewarding.

Organizations need to understand customer service is not an evil expense but rather the lifeline of the organization. The customer's voice has a new person sitting at the highest levels of power in some companies. Whether firms call the position Chief Customer Officer (CCO) or some other label, these individuals serve as top executives with the mandate and power to design, orchestrate, and improve customer "WOW" experiences across the ever-more-complex range of customer interactions. Chief Customer Officers are a relatively new position at the senior executive level which is responsible for making sure the actions of the organization are consistent with what the customer is expecting from the organization. These very senior positions require strong skills in research in addition to general business skills. They welcome change and are looking for ways to make improvements. Every organization no matter the size needs a Chief Customer Officer. These are the people who make sure the "WOWS" happen. While many of these executives hold the title of Chief Customer Officer, others go by names like Chief Client Officer (at OptumHealth), Chief Experience Officer (at Cigna), Executive Vice President, Member Experience (at USAA), or Chief Global Customer and Marketing Officer (at Dunkin' Brands). At smaller organizations, the title could be me, myself or I but the best advice I ever got was "if I could not provide the kind of customer service that is needed and expected hire someone who could." In order to continue growing successfully and providing "WOW" experiences, you need to be more focused on your customers than ever before. Your organizational culture might not be optimal, to say the least. Your operations departments might be too focused on your products and services. Your finance teams might not be structured correctly to meet the customer needs with collecting payments. Your sales and business development teams might not be customer focused meeting short-term revenue goals. Is anyone in your organization looking at things from the customers' perspective?

You may need to change your culture to better serve the one reason we all exist — our customers.

ARE YOU USING THE RIGHT TOOLS?

You want your best customer service people handling problems or as I prefer opportunities. Do you give them the power and influence to resolve situations?

The customer service manager should be a part of the executive management team within the organization. Even if their teams are small, their voice on the executive management team means they have influence over how the company prioritizes and spends resources. Depending on your organization there are several online tools that can help, but you need to be at Step 3 - Conscious Competence State of Thinking to understand how you can influence the "WOW" experience. The tools just provide possible solutions to opportunities, people provide the "WOW".

Using The Right Language can make the difference

What you say can hurt or help you. Your choice of words should not be left up to chance. What we say to customers can have an enormous impact on how customers view us and how we view ourselves. This is where being an unconscious competent makes the difference between good customer service and the "WOW" experience. You cannot leave the choice of words up to your customer service staff. Have a master list for everyone to refer to. When you are consistent, your organization is more likely to communicate the messages it wants others to hear. By choosing words wisely, you can improve the "WOW" experience of your customers and avoid disasters.

Take, for example, "my pleasure" – a signature phrase used by employees of the quick-service restaurant Chick-fil-A – it sure sounds better than "no problem." It subtly reminds employees that service should look as if it is a pleasure and not a chore. The discount department store chain Target refers to its customers as guests. While this may not seem like a big deal, it is. Every time the word guest is used in the store, it is a cue that, indeed, customers are guests and should be treated that way. Disney calls its park employees cast members. This choice in language reinforces the idea that employees are part of the guest experience and are on stage for every visitor to the park. At the University of Michigan, the athletic event staff members are referred to as team members. They are the "face" of Michigan Athletics. On game day they represent the institution in a way that makes everyone proud to be Wolverines.

How do you refer to your customers?

How do you refer to your staff?

Here is a fun exercise you can do to get everyone using the new words the very first day to chance old habits. Get a clear jar and label it the "old words jar" or something like that. Every time a person uses an old word that you want them to change have them throw a quarter in the jar. Make it fun, and every once in a while you can slip up (intentionally of course) and use the wrong word, so you have to throw a quarter into the jar. This helps the process of changing an old habit. Be ready, your staff will kid you for using an old word so just play along. After a couple of weeks use the money from the jar for a donut break and celebrate the improvements everyone has made.

Think about your typical customer service interactions, and look for language opportunities.

What do you call customers?

How do you refer to employees?

How do you say thank you?

Imagine for a moment you are training a new sales person in a retail store. You see one of your regular customers come in. During your introduction, you mention to your new sales person this customer is a business owner in the community, but you neglect to mention they own the local funeral home. Before you can say another word, your new sales person says "glad to meet you how's business? Although a common question to strike up a conversation, in some situations it could be embarrassing or awkward as in this one. We must be consciously aware of what we are saying to every customer.

Here are some new word suggestions but remember the delivery often determines the reaction. Whether it's good news, bad news, or simply passing on information, your choice of words will have a significant effect on the way the customer hears what you're saying. Remember the way they feel about it is how they react to it. The goal, of course, is to create the "WOW" experience.

I am **Delighted** to help

It would be my **Pleasure**

Absolutely

I would be **Happy** to help

I am **Sorry**

I **understand**

Please accept my **apology**

Yes

How may I help you?

Thank you

As a customer would you prefer to hear, I can or I will?

Remember this only works if it's genuine, not forced or scripted. Take a few minutes to review the words and language you use in your organization. Read them out loud and listen to the words as you speak them. Do you hear what you would want to hear as a customer? Sometimes our customers do not understand trade standard words or jargon.

What other words be used in your situation?

Notes:

STEP 2: IDENTIFYING YOUR CUSTOMER

Who are they and what do you know about them

We must make sure we know and use the person's name whenever possible. For first time customers, you should always ask how they would like to be addressed. We should always try to personalize our conversations.

We must know what our customers want before they do and to do this we need to know who they are. We need to understand our customer's perspective. We need to have a conscious understanding and focus on the customer. We can use a number of different methods to finding out who our customers are, but the first and important step is for you to clearly define your organization's objectives, goals, and the unique value you offer your customers. You might be saying to yourself we already do this, great. You're one step ahead.

Now, are they written down and shared with everyone in your organization?

This is a very critical step in being able to create the "WOW" experience.

Take a quick anonymous survey with your customer service representatives. You want to keep the survey anonymous so no one person is singled out and you will also get a more truthful response.

Ask them what is the most important thing your organization has to offer your customers?

The answers you get from this one question will help you identify the diverse culture within your organization. Next, ask them what they know about the customer. We are looking for a common thread that links each customer to the organization.

Customers are not the only stakeholder the organization has, your employees are equally important. It has become more difficult to hire talented new people. For many of our workers, the workplace is not just a place for work; here they develop and maintain some of the most important relationships they have in their life. Our employees are in the day-to-day trenches. They play an important role in your customer service and can provide valuable information about our customers.

How often are the employees asked about their ideas and suggestions?

Some organizations have suggestion boxes or ways to email to a generic mail box. But what I have found is they are seldom used. The best way to find out information is to have a face-to-face discussion with each person. This demonstrates you have a genuine interest just like we train our staff to be with our customers.

People are less willing to keep quiet when they feel an injustice has been done. Organizations cannot afford to just stand by and weather the storm. With the use of social media your organization can be a target and quickly find its self on the wrong end of post or tweet.

No matter what business or organization we are involved in there is always one common thread, the customer. Without customers, we lose our money source.

Customers are our Money Source

"There is only one boss, and whether a person shines shoes for a living or heads up the biggest corporation in the world, the boss remains the same. It is the customer! The customer is the person who pays everyone's salary and who decides whether a business is going to succeed or fail. In fact, the customer can fire everybody in the company from the chairman (CEO) on down, and he can do it simply by spending his money somewhere else. Literally, everything we do, every concept perceived, every technology developed and associate employed, is directed with this one objective clearly in mind – pleasing the customer." Sam M. Walton, CEO Wal-Mart.

Customers provide the revenue we need to operate our organizations. Whether you are in sales, manufacturing, or a nonprofit organization some form of revenue is needed.

Can you identify all your money sources?

What impact would losing one money source have in your organization?

THINKING LIKE OUR CUSTOMERS

Our customers need to know why they should trust us, why they should buy from us, what is so special about our organization compared to the competition, and the benefits of doing business with us. But what they really want to know is how they will feel while doing business with us and after the purchase is made. This is where we want them to have the "WOW" experience. When we think like our customers, we learn to anticipate questions. We can listen between the lines and when possible watch their body language, listen to their tone of voice, or their choice of words. We are consciously looking for ways to create a "WOW" experience. This is where the customer service person needs to know all the ins, and out of the products and services the organization has to offer. They can build upon past experiences and situations.

Everyone likes a bargain and a chance to save a little money. One area that sometimes is a hassle for customers is mail-in rebates.

Here is an example of how one industry teamed up with their suppliers to create a "WOW" experience.

A locally owned and operated hardware store is part of the largest hardware cooperative in the industry. They are known as the helpful hardware store. To stay competitive with the big box stores, their customer service has to be top-notch. Through the use of customer surveys, they established key things their customers were looking for. One thing that many stores have begun to offer their customers is some type of a rewards program based on points per dollar spent system. Although this is nothing new what they have implemented to go along the program is. As a rewards program member, you can instantly redeem rebates at the time of sale. No more mail in the rebate forms, no more waiting to receive the rebate check and no postage cost. Now that is a "WOW" experience. Think about how many 50 cents and $1 coupons you have thrown away because you thought it was not worth the hassle or the cost to mail in for a rebate.

Have you ever called for technical assistance to a company and about half way through the process you hear a click in your ear and you were lost in cyber space forever? Right before you were to get the answer to your question. We all have. Just the other day I was consulting with a client in a similar situation. I suggested at the beginning of the conversation between the customer service person and the customer they should get the best callback number for the customer just in case they are disconnected. The customer service person would inform the customer if they were somehow disconnected they would receive an immediate callback. A small thing like this could make the difference between you and your competition. It could make the difference between keeping a customer or losing a money source. It could even make the difference in getting new customers. You may not see this as a "WOW" experience opportunity, but in your customer's eyes, it just could be. It's the little things that sometimes can make a big difference. This is why we continuously need to be aware of what the customer might be thinking.

Getting feedback from your customers is the best way to measure if we understand who they are. We can use online surveys, mailed surveys and phone surveys.

Notes

Be Aware of Their Needs, Wants, and Desires

Awareness is one of the great differentiators between good service and creating the "WOW" experience. Awareness is noticing the details and looking for the silent problems that go unmentioned. Awareness is an inherently proactive activity. It takes the desire to be "always on" and the courage to look for problems or as I prefer opportunities.

Have you ever heard the saying, "no news is good news"? If you do not hear feedback from your customers every day, you cannot measure and celebrate the successes or possible opportunities in the past and future.

We need to understand what our customer's value the most from our products or services. We need to be flexible with our rules and at the same time be easy to work with.

The action is what our customers want when there is a question or problem. Everyone wants to feel like they are a priority over everything, so we need to recognize this opportunity and meet every want and desire. When we consciously put ourselves in the customer's place, we can see how a "WOW" experience can be a solution.

During the early stages of my customer service career, I was taught to always smile and be cheerful with the customer and never forget the customer was always right, even though sometimes they were wrong. During the mid-1970's I was working as a manager trainee with S.S.Kresge Company better known as Kmart Corporation. During our training sessions, we talked about customer service. The instructors would always tell us stories about how, if the home office ever received a customer complaint from your store, you personally would have to deliver to the customer a box of chocolate candy and a dozen red roses. Of course, all of us young guns took this to be a just urban legend because we never ever knew of anyone who actually experienced the delivery of the candy or roses. Until one day I was working as an assistant manager in a Kmart store. I had been called to the service desk to take care of a merchandise return problem. At this point, the customer was very upset with our customer service desk person because they had refused the customer a refund. Of course, the big Kmart sign hanging above the customer service desk stated "Satisfaction Always, " and in those days you didn't even need to have a sales receipt for a refund. I took all the proper steps to gain control of the situation. I listened to the customer side of the story and was even using the proper body language of nodding my head and showing empathy as we teach our customer service people to do. But then it happened, just as I was about to authorize the refund I noticed the garment which the customer was returning had a JC Penney logo on the identification tag. I was quick to point out to the customer she was in Kmart, not JC Penny's. The customer quickly gathered the garments and left through the front doors. Mad or embarrassed I was not sure. I remember thinking all is well and good. I took a challenging situation with an upset customer and I was able to resolve the problem, or so I thought. The next day I got called into the store manager's office. He asked me a few questions about the customer service problem the day before. I explained to him what had happened and that in fact, the customer was at the wrong store. He quickly corrected me and said no the customer was at the right store, our store and this is where we need all customers to be, in our store. He was quick to remind me that we were in competition with all retail stores and if we wanted to continue to be successful, we needed to satisfy as many customers as possible. That is why the Kmart slogan is "Satisfaction Guaranteed." I sensed the urban legend was about to become true and I was right. I was instructed to go to the local flower shop and get a dozen red roses and on my way out of the store stop by the candy department and get a box of chocolates. I only had a few dollars in my pocket until the next pay period which was about a week away. I wasn't sure where I was going to get the money to pay for the roses. So I called a friend of mine who worked at one of the local florists, and he helped me out. I arrived at the customer's house and explain how truly sorry I was and presented her with a box of chocolate candy and a dozen red roses. The customer accepted my apology and said wow the box of chocolate candy and the dozen red roses were not necessary but greatly appreciated. The next pay period came, and I settle my debts, and I thought to myself this was an expensive lesson. A couple of weeks had passed when I received a handwritten thank you note from the customer. I immediately took the note to the store manager and showed him. With a big smile and a pat on my back, he said congratulations a job well done. In my next paycheck, there was a handwritten note from the store manager. Once again, congratulating me on a job well done and to my surprise, there was included the money for the box of chocolate candy and the dozen red roses along with a bonus for providing good customer service. This is how I began to understand the power of the "WOW" experience.

Step 3: Creating the "WOW" EXPERIENCE

Managing Customer Expectations every Moment of Every day

A favorable first impression sets the stage for the "WOW" experience. You begin providing service the moment a customer comes into your business, calls you on the telephone, or e-mails you. Without even thinking, they form a first impression. How you speak, how well you listen, the words you choose, and how you write and respond using e-mail all contribute to first impressions. If a customer's first impression is favorable, you have laid the foundation for providing great customer service and the "WOW" experience.

We need to exceed and do the unexpected whenever possible. When we make commitments to our customers, we must deliver on those commitments. We must take personal responsibility for every situation. We must earn our customers trust. This is essential to retaining and gaining customers.

Here is a fun exercise to do with your customer service staff. As individuals have them write down the steps of their job. Next in teams have them brainstorm how each individual step could be presented as a "WOW" experience.

Remember the rules for brainstorming:

The words "Stupid Idea" can never be used

Defer judgment – separating idea generation from idea selection strengthens both activities. For now, suspend critique. Know that you'll have plenty of time to evaluate the ideas after the brainstorm session.

Encourage wild ideas – breakout ideas are right next to the absurd ones-remember we are looking for "WOW" experiences.

Build on the ideas of others – listen and add to the flow of ideas. These will springboard your group to places no individual can get to on their own

Go for quantity – best way to have a good idea is to have lots of ideas

One conversation at a time – maintain momentum as a group. Save the side conversations for later.

Headline – capture the essence quickly and move on. Don't stall the group by going into a long-winded idea.

Remember - Brainstorming sessions are worthless unless ideas lead to action!

Think about the last time you were in a brainstorming session. What ever happened to the ideas and suggestions? Where they ever used or did you think it was a waste of time?

Do not let this happen. Make a list of the ideas and suggestions that everyone has brainstormed. Prioritize them in the order of importance and evaluate how these ideas might fit into your short and long term goals. See how they will help make "WOW" experiences. Then share with everyone how the new ideas will be implemented. Keep the list visible for everyone to see and mark the date when the idea was used and what the result was.

Taking Action - Situation, Evaluation, and Analysis

Any list of needed customer service skills is bound to be incomplete. Customer service and customer experience management incorporate operational, technological, and interpersonal skills that are as diverse as they are numerous. Regardless of the industry, these basic skills almost universally apply to any "WOW" experience.

Most customer service positions are within companies that have official ways of handling problems. You will need to be able to not just look over the rules but actually, internalize them. This is where Unconscious Competence State of Thinking is the most important. This is your ability to use protocol and guidelines .You need to understand the guidelines and then use them the way they are intended.

Problem Solving-"WOW" experiences are all about problem-solving even when there is not a problem. Finding the glitches in your customer experience and the ways to fix them is an example of proactive problem-solving. The reactive problem solving is how to make an unhappy customer happy within the bounds of your authority. Solving problems, before and after they occur, is at the heart of the "WOW" experience.

Strategic Preparation -In almost any organization, the "WOW" experience is only as good as the systems that support it. Knowing how to break down the customer journey and prepare to deliver service excellence at each point along the way is a crucial skill to have.

Active Listening - If a customer service representative is not listening to the customer they are never going to be able to provide great service. Not only do you need to be able to hear what they are telling you in terms of sheer data, but you also need to be able to try to understand what they mean by what they are saying. Applying this skill means you care enough to put effort into providing verbal and nonverbal feedback to the person speaking, feedback that tells them you are listening and are focused on what they are saying. Nodding your head, making commentary to emphasize their points, and maintaining good eye contact all signal to the listener that what they have to say is important. In today's digitally distracted world, listening is becoming an increasingly rare skill. Of course, people speak at different speeds. Some take longer to get to the point, and some never get to a point at all. But if they are your customer, they deserve not only to be heard but to be paid attention to. And eye contact means the person, not your iPhone. The opposite of talking isn't listening. The opposite of talking is waiting.

Clear Verbal Communication-we need to be able to communicate verbally with the customer. The purpose of this kind of communication is to not just repeat information to the customer but to make sure that they understood what you said. You will need proper speaking skills, good grammar, and the ability to choose the right mode of speaking, and the correct words for the person on the other end of the line or across the counter from you.

Empathy - is the ability to relate to how someone is feeling, to understand what they are going through. We attempt to put ourselves in their place. Empathy is sensing and understanding the emotions of others and of all the customer service skills, some will argue that this is most important. Those who are good at empathy can often win the trust of even the most dissatisfied customers because those customers will feel they have someone on their side. You need to be able to listen and actually involve yourself in what the customer is telling you about their situation. If you are only following policy and not listening (Step 1 Unconscious Incompetence State of Thinking) you may miss important special considerations that need to be taken into account in order for customer service to be kept at a high-quality level allowing for the "WOW" experience.

I was consulting with an owner of a restaurant who was having difficulties with their customer service. While talking with the wait staff, the topic of tips kept coming to the front of the discussion but nothing about customer service. The restaurant was equipped with a point-of-sale terminal, which allowed the wait staff to force the tip on every transaction. The wait staff thought this was a good idea to force tips on each transaction so they would be guaranteed their tips every time. This was our first day of meeting, and it was clear they were in stage one being unconscious incompetence. After meeting with the restaurant owner, I suggested working with a couple of wait staff personnel that were considered the leaders. I knew if I could demonstrate some quick results the other wait staff team members would quickly respond. As we were talking about customer service, everyone believed they had the best service in town. I asked them what the one thing was that made them better than any other restaurant in town. Yes, you guessed it they all had a different answer. I then asked everyone what was the last "WOW" experience at a restaurant they had gone to as a customer? No one could recall any recent positive experiences just bad experiences.

After a little coaching, I had prepared the leaders of the wait staff to provide a "WOW" experience for their customers. Before they had a chance to use these new found skills, I wanted to provide them with a "WOW" experience of their own. Because the tip policy was one of their main concerns, I offered them this guarantee. If they would just try the ideas, I suggested I would guarantee their tips for their shift. They did not have to worry about forcing tips or how much money they would be earning. I just wanted them to concentrate on the "WOW" experience for their customers. At the end of each of their shifts when they closed out their sales their tips had exceeded what they would have earned if they forced the tips on each Check. This "WOWED" each one of them. By providing the "WOW" experience to each of their customers, they were rewarded with good tips. They got a double "WOW" when I told them they got to keep the difference between what they thought they were going to earn and what they actually earned. Now everyone received the "WOW" experience. The remaining employees were eager to learn.

Notes:

Notes:

Rewarding

We need to catch people doing things well and acknowledge it.

Providing "WOW" experiences is in its self is a rewarding experience. There is no substitute for the feeling you get when your customer has a "WOW" experience and thank you.

In order to have a satisfied customer, you start with a satisfied employee. Employees have an intrinsic need for appreciation, respect, motivation and challenging work. Appreciation is linked to employee performance. Rewards provide immediate recognition which is critical to demonstrate superior work. Your reward system can be very simple or more formally structured. It depends on what works for your organization and budget. If you don't have any employees, it's still important to reward yourself.

The most important thing to remember is you must be consistent with your rewarding system. You cannot go gangbusters for a couple of weeks and then start scaling it back. It won't work.

You first need to design and set up your reward program. Your time frame should be specific with measurable goals. For example, the very first day you begin I would have the "old words jar" ready and explain to everyone how it works. Then give everyone a list of new words with a few examples how to use them and let the fun begin. To help get things started to be the first person to use an old word and throw a quarter in the jar. This will help break the ice. Keep in mind no one wants to make the first mistake. Let your staff police themselves and have fun with it.

Make sure you reward all the successes through the Conscious Competence Ladder of Learning. Don't wait for the "WOW" experiences to happen to begin rewarding. By knowing what motivates your people, you can implement a system that really will make your team feel more appreciated. Reward Individual performance as well as Team performance.

You can have your employees nominate people within their team who have exceeded the expectations and gone above and beyond creating the "WOW" experience.

In my opinion, there is a difference between recognition and financial reward, but many organizations try to link the two together. Take a look at the reward system within your organization.

How do you feel about it?

How do others feel about it?

What additions or changes would you make?

No two organizations are the same, so your recognition program will vary with your organizational culture. There is no perfect formula so don't wait, get started today. Start by telling people just how good they are doing and how you appreciate their effort. Share their success with others.

Some popular items for rewards. Are t-shirts with special sayings, coffee mugs, and special pins. These items could be for your weekly or monthly goals. Daily rewards could be hand written notes to each individual or a tally board listing the successes achieved. Get everyone involved and find out what they would value as a reward. Don't be stingy with your rewards. The goal is to get everyone engaged as quickly as possible and experience success.

You can never give employees too much positive recognition. Make sure you are authentic and not automatic. We need to celebrate each and every "WOW" experience that is created.

Make a List of Some Possible Rewards

Follow-up

There is a need to create clarity for all employees regarding customer service quality policies and customer satisfaction targets when implementing the "WOW" experience. It is not enough to pay lip-service to these ideals and to expect success in attaining them. The starting point must be to identify what has to be achieved in customer satisfaction to implement specific market strategies, and to position the company against the competition in a specific market. It is unlikely that achieving what is needed will be free from cost. We need to take a realistic view of the time needed and the real costs of implementation in aligning the internal market with the external market.

Internal processes and barriers suggest the need to consider both the internal and external markets faced in implementing customer satisfaction measurement and management systems. To ignore the internal market is to risk actually damaging the company's capacity to achieve and improve customer satisfaction in the external market.

If for example, management uses customer feedback in a negative and coercive way, then it may reduce employee enthusiasm for customer service, or create 'game-playing' behavior where people compete for 'Brownie points' in the system at the expense of both the company and the customer. This said, we have also to recognize not just the complementarity between internal and external markets, but the potential for conflict of interest. Achieving target levels of customer service and satisfaction may require managers and employees to change the way they do things and to make sacrifices they do not want to make. This may take more than simple advocacy or management threat.

Related to the above argument, recognizing the internal market suggests that there may be a need for a structured and planned internal customer service program to achieve the effective implementation of customer satisfaction measurement and management. This has been described as marketing our customers to our employees and can be built into the implementation process to address the needs of the internal customer and to confront the types of internal procession barrier we have encountered. Other departments might not support you "WOW" experiences approach to customer service. They may not recognize the need or benefits.

Also related to the recognition of the internal market is the need to question the relationship between internal and external customer satisfaction. This can be discussed with executives using the structure shown in Figure 1. This suggests four possible scenarios that result when internal and external customer satisfaction are compared:

(a) Synergy, which is what we hope for, when internal and external customer satisfaction are high, and we see them as sustainable and self-regenerating. As one hotel manager explained it: 'I know that we are winning on customer service when my operational staff come to me and complain about how I am getting in their way in providing customer service, and tell me to get my act together!' This is the 'happy customers and happy employees' situation, assumed by many to be obvious and easily achieved.

(b) Coercion is where we achieve high levels of external customer satisfaction by changing the behavior of employees through management direction and control systems. In the short term, this may be the only option, but it may be very difficult and expensive to sustain this position in the longer term, and we give up flexibility for control.

(c) Alienation is where we have low levels of satisfaction internally and externally, and we are likely to be highly vulnerable to competitive attack on service quality, and to the instability in our competitive capabilities produced by low staff morale and high staff turnover.

(d) Internal euphoria is where we have high levels of satisfaction in the internal market, but this does not translate into external customer satisfaction – for example, if internal socialization and group cohesiveness actually shut out the paying customer in the external market. These scenarios are exaggerated but have provided a useful way of confronting these issues with employees and managers.

A critical mistake is to ignore the real costs and challenges of sustaining high service quality levels and the limitation which may exist in a company's capabilities for improving customer satisfaction levels. While advocacy is widespread and the appeal is obvious, achieving the potential benefits requires more planning and attention to implementation realities than is suggested by the existing conventional literature.

Final Thoughts

If this was easy, then everyone would be providing "WOW" experiences, and you would not need this book. Change alone is difficult but to suggest "WOW" experiences every time could be a set-up for failure unless there is a clear understanding what it takes each time we interact with people. Sure there will be trying times during the learning process, but the results will be priceless and rewarding. This is your call to action. Only you can decide what your next step will be. Have fun making the "WOW" experience happen for everyone you interact with.

ABOUT THE AUTHOR

Dr. James Ortman has been involved with customer service since 1974. Dr. Ortman teaches marketing and management related subjects at several universities. He is always smiling and looking for ways to take every customer service situation to the next level. He believes success comes in forms of "I can rather than I cannot."

www.ingramcontent.com/pod-product-compliance
Lightning Source LLC
Chambersburg PA
CBHW071255170526
45165CB00003B/1352